# The Wise Mind of H.I.M. Emperor Haile Sellassie I

Foreword: H.I.H. Prince Ermias Sahle Selassie
Introduction: Ras Sekou S. Tafari

© Frontline Distribution Int'l Inc. & Research Associates
School Times Publication 2018

*First Printing: 2004*
*Second Printing: 2007*
*Third Printing: 2012*
*Fourth Printing: 2017*
*Fifth Printing: 2018*
*Fifth Printing: 2022*

ISBN #: 9780948390869
Library of Congress #: 2009944095

Print Coordinator: Prizgar G.
Book Cover Design Concept: Cathy LaShea
Book Cover Design & Page Layout: Ras Tzaddi Wadadah II

T0019977

# TABLE OF CONTENTS

# Foreword

We are fortunate indeed that so many of His Imperial Majesty, Haile Sellassie's words have been saved. Many documents were destroyed during the Communist revolution (1974-1975), which vainly tried to erase 3,500 years of tradition. However, so great is the international legacy of His Majesty that many records were preserved by a grateful world, including his speeches during the period 1930 to 1974.

These speeches are remarkable in that they provide a vivid panorama, through His Majesty's eyes, of the problems and challenges confronting a young Ethiopian king: national development, foreign aggression and invasion, war and resistance, foreign relations, and so on. The sheer volume of the speeches made over nearly half a century may make it difficult for the ordinary reader to examine. This is why I undertook excerpting from His Majesty's speeches, some of my favourite quotations and organized them into this book. These were selected in many cases because of their historic significance. Some became the basis for many modern expressions that have entered mainstream Western popular culture, such as the cry, "No justice, no peace" of the American civil rights movement or the music of Jamaican reggae artist, Bob Marley. But, in every case, they were selected because the values and lessons are eternal and useful.

Besides offering a rare historical perspective, His Majesty's remarks reveal not only his singular character, but also a window into a confluence of ancient cultural and intellectual resources. His childhood was, of course, deeply affected by his parents and family. The values they imparted unto him had been passed from generation to generation since King Solomon and even beyond to ancient Egypt and Ethiopia. Foremost among these were a love of justice and learning.

Ethiopia was the world's first Christian nation. The role of its Royal Family and the Ethiopian Orthodox Church has historically been closely intertwined. The young Ras Tafari was devoutly religious and, no doubt, it was though the church that he formed his strong faith and sense of the immediacy of God in daily life.

From illustrious ancestors, such as King Menelik, whom His Majesty would one day erect an impressive monument; His Imperial Majesty, Haile Sellassie, learned pride and love of country. He had been born shortly before the battle of Adowa, in which the triumph of Ethiopia over the technologically superior Italian colonialists represented a crack in the paradigm of European supremacy over the people of colour. In this atmosphere, his early worldview was infused with fierce independence and courage.

His Majesty's formal education was supervised by Jesuits. Known for a rigorous method of logical analysis, their instruction provided an invaluable mental tool that aided the future King in the analysis of, and deep insight into, complex and highly nuanced problems.

His Majesty was also a keen observer of human nature and the natural environment. He was later to remark that there are many things one can learn from the people. Such observations certainly contributed to an unyielding common sense and appreciation of the value of hard work. This trait, added to the other values described above, gave His Majesty the rare ability to apply his philosophy and deep understanding to practical concerns.

Finally, of course, there is the mystery of personality and history, that transcendent spark that enable these disparate elements to come together uniquely at a critical juncture in time and space. To see millennia of varied strands of human thought and experience synthesized in one man just when the fate of a continent hung in the balance, is to see the hand of God.

This book was prepared in order to make this wisdom more accessible. If it is not only read but also studied, contemplated and, ultimately, heeded, both the reader, society at large and future generations will benefit.

H.I.H Prince Ermias Sahle Selassie
Washington, DC
March 2004

# 1ˢᵗ, 2ⁿᵈ and 3ʳᵈ Edition's Introduction

*Today men hope for a peaceful future, when yesterday we sought only the means to postpone the final holocaust.*

*If the condition of peace is such as will satisfy the conscience and sense of justice of men, if it is assured to humankind that they shall toil and live happily in a just system in which no discrimination will be made between small and great, the peace system that shall be laid down can leave a heritage for the coming generation which will be a full of happy life and boundless prosperity.*

*Man is basically a creature of peace. Use your knowledge for good, to preserve peace among men.*

*- Emperor Haile Sellassie I*

It is in times like this, in a time of wars and rumours of wars; a time when the AIDS epidemic is spreading uncontrollably throughout Southern Africa (Azania), and other parts of our glorious African continent like a thief in the night. It is in times like this when people in Africa and other underdeveloped countries, such as Haiti, are still living below the United Nations' defined poverty level. It is in these times, that reflection on *The Wise Mind of Emperor Haile Sellassie I* of Ethiopia can become very pertinent in our daily lives.

Emperor Haile Sellassie I was deposed in a palace coup led by Colonel Mengistu in 1974. Haile Sellassie I was very pertinacious about not resisting this coup.

*"Firmly, Haile Sellassie I declared that he did not wish to see the shedding of blood, and that he would never again give orders that could have that result. While still in possession of power, he surrendered without a fight. This was a battle he did not want to win.[1]"*

[1] Hans Wilhelm Lockot, *The Mission: The Life, Reign & Character of Haile Sellassie I* (Chicago: Frontline Distribution International, 2001), 121.

Emperor Haile Sellassie I was the last reigning monarch of Ethiopia. He came from a line of monarchs that can be traced beyond the union of Queen Makeda, of Sheba, a province in Ethiopia, and King Solomon of Israel. Ethiopia has a very rich history. Ethiopia was once described as the Mother of ancient Egypt-Kemet.

The speeches compiled in *The Wise Mind of Haile Sellassie I* were selected and edited by his grandson, Prince Ermias Sahle Selassie of the Ethiopian Royal Council.

Throughout his reign as Regent, King and finally Emperor, Haile Sellassie I managed to take Ethiopia from feudalism to a modern-day state. During his reign as Emperor, which commenced formally on November 2, 1930, many Africans, both in the west and in Africa, saw H.I.M. as their spokesperson against colonialism. Haile Sellassie I was a very wise and astute man. He was very clever and diligent when deliberating on matters of world affairs, spirituality, African independence, education, etc. as it relates to Ethiopia and other African countries. He spoke out very candidly:

*"Africa has been reborn as a free continent and Africans have been reborn as free men. The blood that was shed and the sufferings that were endured are today Africa's advocates for freedom and unity. The glories and advantages of freedom cannot be purchased with all the world's material wealth.[2]"*

Haile Sellassie I, Emperor of Ethiopia from 1930 to 1974, was an active champion of African independence, African unity and Africa's modern development. He often defended the rights of the poor and suffering nations of the world, firstly at the League of Nations and later at the United Nations.

This selection of writings and speeches of this colossal African giant should impact our daily lives. These excerpts should act as a catalyst for many of us, especially those young people who didn't experience this African King and Emperor in their lifetime.

---

[2] Hans Wilhelm Lockot, *The Mission: The Life, Reign & Character of Haile Sellassie I* (Chicago: Frontline Distribution International, 2001), 122.

Emperor Haile Sellassie I meant different things to various people. Many Christians and members of the Ethiopian Orthodox church saw him as the defender of the faith. To others, he was literally King of Kings, and the Lord of Lords, of Ethiopia, and the world, in accordance with the New Testament. To others, he was the Christ returned after two thousand years in a Kingly character. Then to others, like the Rastafari Movement, who adopted his name, he is the incarnation of the Creator, the living God manifesting in human flesh.

However, Haile Sellassie I, the last reigning monarch of Ethiopia in the 20th century, left a very remarkable legacy as a monument for the world. His speeches and actions can and should be used as a black print in conjunction with the likes of Marcus Garvey, Kwame Nkrumah, Amilcar Cabral, Malcolm X, etc., so as to advance the cause of the African race and mankind overall.

We must put to the best use the rich heritage of our past for, in that way, and in that way alone can we live to the highest standard set by our forefathers.

We hope the future generations will realize the magnitude of sacrifices that was required to accomplish all the works, so that it may preserve it as gain.

This book, *The Wise Mind of Emperor Haile Sellassie I*, is a vital reading for the development of all mankind.

It is very inspirational, very motivational, very educational, very philosophical, and a very fulfilling handbook. *The Wise Mind of Emperor Haile Sellassie I* should be read daily. It can become a magnificent tool for elevating one's mind, body, and soul in the 21st century and beyond.

The African struggle continues!
Ras Sekou Sankara Tafari
March 2004

# 4th Special Edition Introduction

> *"Throughout history, it has been the inaction of those who could have acted; the indifference of those who should have known better; the silence of the voice of justice when it mattered most; that has made it possible for evil to triumph."*
>
> - The I Majesty Haile Sellassie I

It is now approaching thirteen years since we, at Frontline Books, collaborated with Prince Ermias, the grandson of Haile Sellassie I—the last reigning emperor of Ethiopia—to issue this book now known to the world as, *The Wise Mind of Emperor Haile Sellassie I* (TWM). This book has been accepted and endorsed publicly by many of our elders and our young Rastafari cultural ambassadors, such as Jah9, Chronixx, Protoje, and most recently, Khari Kill; who did the first dub plate, which highlighted the serious need for all to read.

Since *The Wise Mind* came into existence, we have seen crucial years in the growth and expansion of the Rastafari Nation worldwide. On the global stage, we saw the emergence of the first so-called Black President of the United States of America, a great and remarkable feat for, Africans living in the Americas and for Diasporic Africans, in general.

Within the last two years, the passing of legislation in the Caribbean island of Jamaica decriminalized cannabis, making Jamaica the only country in the world where the plant can be legally used as sacrament. This was a great reform and progressive step by the government of Jamaica on behalf of the Rastafari community.

As we review these years, the evolution of a new writ of Rastafari is being formulated. Our esteemed and great noble-patriarch, Ras Mortimer Planno, initiated the call some years ago for the need from within the Rastafari nation, to write, "...a new faculty of interpretation of Rastafari." As more youths in the inner cities, are growing their hair into locks, all around the world, many are showing a keen interest in Rastafari culture and its livity. Some are now asking the pertinent question—What is Rastafari?

I was showing my beloved brethren, Tzaddi Ayoung Wadada I, one of the new features that our anniversary editor, Asheda Dwyer, proposed. After reading an excerpt, he said to me, "Ras! It is reading like the Bible." To most ears, that statement can be received as a great compliment. However, I now ask these questions—What is the Bible? And does the Bible set the standard for us as Rastafari and how we should live in the year 2017 and beyond?

At this junction in our history, we are now faced with this vital question: Did God make man or did man make God? Part of this answer lies here in *The Ruins of Empire* by C.F Volney:

> *"Ah! Now I know the lying spirit of man! Contemplating the picture which he had drawn of the Divinity: No said I, it is not God who had made man after the image of God, but man hath made God after the image of man; he hath given him his own mind, clothed him with his own propensities, ascribed to him his own judgments. And when in this medley, he finds the contradiction of his own principles, with hypocritical humility, he imputes weakness to his reason, and names the absurdities of his own mind the mysteries of God. He hath*

*said God is immutable, yet he offers prayers to change him; he hath pronounced him incomprehensible, yet he interprets him without ceasing.[3]"*

The King James Bible, or, *The Book of the Rib-and-the-Ribless* (as it is referred to by our youthful, Rastafari scholar, Asheda Dwyer) is for the most part, a book of European-interpreted myths and mythos. "Yes!" the I Majesty Haile Sellassie I, pinpoints "...for myself, I glory in the Bible." However, it is important to assert that for centuries, the Holy Bible has been used as a weapon to dehumanize and demoralize African people as less than human.

It is this book that helped make the feminine human species—the woman—into an inferior human being. In the New Testament, according to Paul (also known as Saul), "man is head of the woman, just as Christ is head of the church." In addition, when we review the *so-called* Genesis story, it relates Eve in the form of a

---

[3] Constantin-Francois de Volney, *The Ruins of Empire* (Baltimore: Black Classic Press, 1991), 78.

woman, as the one responsible for encouraging
Adam, the first man, to commit the first sin. Let
us delve further and expand Rastafari, whereby
the genders, though biologically different,
realize that we are indeed all equal as fellow
human beings. This would follow the example
of our mother Menen and our father Haile
Sellassie I, thus practicing one of the principles
of Ancient Africa, "As above, so below".

Of course, *The Wise Mind* is not a bible, but
it may become more relevant in today's world
than a book filled with European myths that
does not relate to us as African people. It is most
relevant and applicable to our immediate
conditions of continued racial suppression and
disunity amongst African states, and amongst us
as African people.

*The Wise Mind* affords us positive
affirmations that can help elevate us from the
bowels of this hopeless, capitalist-imperialist,
racist-shitstem that we are forced to exist. When
read critically, *The Wise Mind* replaces a false,
pale-skin mythical Jesus with a new living
reality—Haile Sellassie I, the most progressive
of the Ethiopian monarchs. *The Wise Mind*
continues to contribute to this new faculty of
Rastafari interpretation that is constantly

evolving. However, this evolution will be shaped throughout time and space, as our young nation continues to grow worldwide.

Nonetheless, during the last decade plus, we have seen qualitative shifts within Rastafari as a way of life. More than before, both Empress Menen and Emperor Haile Sellassie I are now declared and lauded simultaneously, especially by our youthful Rastafari nation. As we strive to find balance, most Rastafari youths see both Menen and the I Majesty as the fulfillment of this practical trinity with the Rastafari nation concluding its manifestation. Thus, we have: father, mother and child—the original trinity formation.

Let us arm ourselves: every man, woman and youth of the African Diaspora with this anniversary edition. The sayings and quotations therein, are suitable for us to apply in our daily lives at this time. The astro-theological myths of Solomon, David, Joshua, Abraham, Ham, etc. are irrelevant to us when anti-black racism is alive, kicking and killing our young men and women in the form of white police execution worldwide. Especially in the so-called democratic United States of America, just as it was in the old, southern, Jim Crow days, as in the days of the colonial, buckeye-master in the British-Caribbean, and so on.

As members of a new race, let us eradicate further the vestiges of colonialism and neo-colonialism by pulling down the pale image of Michael Angelo uncle's portraits that continue to hang on the walls in verandas and homes in the Caribbean, Africa, Asia, Europe, South, Central and North America. It is about time we pull these portraits and ideologies down, and destroy them. Let us denounce racial discrimination in all forms. As the I Majesty profoundly said:

> *"Until the Philosophy which holds one race superior and another inferior is finally and permanently discredited and abandoned; Until there are no longer first-class and second-class citizens of any nation; Until the colour of a man's skin is of no more significance than the colour of his eyes; Until the basic human rights are equally guaranteed to all without regard to race; Until that day, the*

*dream of lasting    peace    and    world
citizenship and the rule of international
morality will remain but a   fleeting
illusion   to   be   pursued   but   never
attained...[4]"*

We   must   uphold   the   anti-colonial   and
revolutionary spirit of *The Wise Mind* by
striving for global unification of Africans in this
ongoing struggle for full justice and human
rights in this brutal Armageddon.

Father Haile Sellassie I and Mother Menen
are satisfied.

The African Liberation Struggle continues…

Ready for Liberation!
Ras Sekou S. Tafari
Chicago, USA
January, 2016

---

[4] Haile Sellassie, "United Nations General Assembly
18<sup>th</sup> Session: 1229<sup>th</sup> Plenary Meeting" (New York:
Online Database System, 1963), 3.
http://daccessddsny.un.org/doc/UNDOC/GEN/NL6/3
03/10/PDF/NL630310.pdf?OpenElement
(accessed January 28th, 2016).

# Chapter 1 – Peace

**1.1** Peace is the foundation for development.

**1.2** The flower of peace is not sustained by poverty, and want.

**1.3** Peace is a day-to-day problem, the product of a multitude of events and judgements. Peace is not an is — it is a becoming.

**1.4** Unless the desire for peace is expressed in terms of concrete achievements and thus gives a sense of assurance and serenity to humanity, mere pious hope constitutes only self-delusion.

**1.5** The essential prerequisite for economic and social contentment is world peace, and without such contentment, the weeds of discontent luxuriate, and threats of peace develop.

**1.6** The great nations of the world would do well to remember that in the modern age, even their own fates are not wholly in their hands. Peace demands the united efforts of us all.

**1.7** Where there is no lack of goodwill, all international disputes can be resolved...all nations, whatever their political persuasions, can live together in peace.

**1.8** Peaceful coexistence is not merely the absence of war...the word itself is an empty bottle; it is for us to give it content and meaning.

**1.9** Peace…has become even more necessary to mankind than ever before. The alternatives confronting the governments of today are no longer peace or war, but peace or the annihilation and complete doom of mankind.

**1.10** It has now become the noble responsibility of Christians and peoples of other faiths and their leaders throughout the world to pray and to work hard for the preservation of world peace.

**1.11** Memories of past injustice should not divert us from the more pressing business at hand. We must live in peace with our former colonizers, shunning recrimination and bitterness and foreswearing the luxury of vengeance and retaliation, lest the acid of hatred erode our souls and poison our hearts.

**1.12** Let us act as befits of dignity, which we claim for ourselves as Africans, proud of our own special qualities, distinctions and abilities.

**1.13** Our efforts as free men must be to establish new relationships, devoid of any resentment and hostility, restored to our belief and faith in ourselves as individuals, dealing on a basis of equality with other equally free people.

**1.14** We desire nothing but peace and the opportunity quietly and without hindrance to march along the path of progress.

**1.15** The teachings of the Gospel in Africa…in the past centuries…has served as a guiding factor and instrument for the freedom and independence now enjoyed by many Africans throughout the continent. As St. Paul said, "Where the Spirit of the Lord is, there is Liberty."

**1.16** The responsibility for safeguarding world peace is not limited to the great powers. Peace and war affect not only the big powers but all mankind, and are therefore the concern of all peoples of the world.

**1.17** We must ensure that disputes in Africa are settled peacefully. If our continent is not free from internecine strife, how can we hope to influence others whose disputes endanger the peace of the world?

**1.18** Never fail to reflect the patient faith of all peoples that only through discussion, collaboration, agreement, and enforcement of the will of mankind - can world peace and stability be achieved.

**1.19** The preservation of peace and the guaranteeing of man's basic freedoms and rights

3

require courage and eternal vigilance: courage to speak and act, and if necessary, to suffer and die for truth and justice.

**1.20** Eternal vigilance [is the principle] that the least transgression of international morality shall not go undetected and unremedied. These lessons must be learned anew by each succeeding generation, and that generation is fortunate indeed, which learns from its own bitter experience.

**1.21** Warfare has never made and can never make an affirmative contribution to the welfare of mankind; good cannot grow out of evil.

**1.22** The life of the world is such that periods of constructive achievement are followed by periods of destruction; the period of construction brings peace and the period of destruction brings uncertainty.

**1.23** In the pondering over the life, the goodness, humility and sacrifice of the saviour of the world, in looking at the laws which he gave us, how much should we be ashamed to call ourselves Christian people, and yet not to follow in his footsteps?

**1.24** Had we been Christian people, had we been worthy of the name, peace would have reigned on all the face of the earth, and would have risen to the level of those immortal angels who always glorify the eternal God, and the peoples of the world would no longer remain divided into hostile camps.

**1.25** War and rumours of war are occupying the attention of governments and peoples, but the world is thirsting more than ever for peace and justice.

**1.26** The flames of war have not for a moment ceased to flicker from point to point across the world.

**1.27** There is enough hunger and misery in the world without further war and suffering.

**1.28** The vast sums swallowed by modern arsenals capable of infinite destruction could be employed in providing food for hungry mouths, in eradicating poverty, illiteracy and disease, in building for a united world the better way of life which man's genius has made it possible.

**1.29** Let us vow to be strong today only that we may, in our strength, advance the time when it will be possible to beat our swords into ploughshares, and when nation shall not make war upon nation. Let Us pledge together that this time will not be long.

**1.30** Let us work for trust among men, for disarmament, for peace.

**1.31** I do not think Italy has enriched her history, illustrious in other ways, by sending her sons to massacre Ethiopians; or that her economy will derive, by her brutal methods or exploiting my country, more profit than she could have derived by a loyal collaboration with a peaceful Ethiopia.

**1.32** Disarmament has become the urgent imperative of our time. l do not say this because I equate the absence of arms to peace, or because I believe that bringing an end to the nuclear arms race automatically guarantees peace, or because the elimination of nuclear warheads from the arsenals of the world will bring in its wake that change in attitude requisite to the peaceful settlement of disputes between nations.

**1.33** Disarmament is vital today, quite simply, because of the immense destructive capacity of which men dispose.

**1.34** Conflicts between nations will continue to arise. The real issue is whether they are to be resolved by force, or by resort to peaceful methods and procedures, administered by impartial institutions.

**1.35** Unless peaceful solutions are devised, counsels of moderation will avail for naught.

**1.36** The major challenges confronting the world today are two: the preservation of peace and the betterment of the living conditions of that half of the world which is poor. These are, of course, mutually interdependent.

**1.37** Without peace, it is futile to talk of improving man's lot: and without such improvement, the task of guaranteeing peace is rendered manifold more difficult. The assault on these two problems must be made simultaneously, and all of our actions should be taken with an eye to the solution of both.

**1.38** Were a real and effective disarmament achieved and the funds now spent in the arms race devoted to the amelioration of man's state; were we to concentrate only on the peaceful uses of nuclear knowledge, how vastly and in how short a time might be changed the conditions of mankind. This should be our goal.

**1.39** There is no doubt that the wealth wasted in the destruction of human could, if properly utilized, have contributed enormously towards the welfare of men and the worldwide advancement of civilization.

**1.40** Contrary to certain notions that the preservation of world peace is the exclusive preserve of the great powers, the question of peace or war, because it involves the survival of humanity, is one that is intimately and vitally connected with all the peoples of the world.

**1.41** When we talk of the equality of man, we find, also, a challenge and an opportunity ... a challenge to breathe new life into the ideals enshrined in the charter, an opportunity to bring men closer to freedom and true equality, and thus, closer to a love of peace.

**1.42** Distant worlds have been brought closer and mysteries have been unfolded. All these achievements should have brought satisfaction to mankind. However, [humanity] among other things, has used these great achievements to evil ends.

**1.43** The realization that such a state of affairs is incompatible with the needs of our times has led, of late, all leaders and all men goodwill to determine to live in peace and to coexist in spite of the ideological, social and economic differences existing in the world.

**1.44** It is, therefore, the sacred duty of all to take advantage of the recent general detente and to strive to bring about enduring peace so that we may spare ourselves the condemnation of posterity and history.

**1.45** We have on numerous occasions declared our nation's devoted respect for the rights of others, non-interference in the internal affairs of states respect for the territorial integrity and sovereignty of nations, the peaceful settlement of disputes, support of the principle of collective security as the best protection against aggression and the best guardian of the peace.

**1.46** To live in peace and friendship with all men today, it is only necessary that these principles find the universal observance which we have so long urged...

**1.47** The way to peace among men and nations rests in the even-handed application and enforcement of the principles of the United Nations and the Organization of African Unity...

**1.48** As long as there are men who believe that one race is superior to the other and that they can lead the destinies of other men by any means, there shall be no peace.

**1.49** [With] groundless irredentism and interference in other states' internal affairs, there [will be] no...peace.

**1.50** It is only by adhering to the principles set out in the Charters of the United Nations and the Organisation of African Unity that we can achieve our aims and that our unity will grow stronger.

**1.51** The greatest disturbance that may be caused in relations among peoples is the confirmation and consecration of a violation of right and law, homage paid to the aggressor, the sacrifice of a victim.

**1.52** To win the war, to overcome the enemy upon the field, cannot alone ensure the victory in peace. The cause of war must be removed. Each nation's rights must be secure from violation.

**1.53** Above all, from the human mind, must be erased all thoughts of war as a solution. Then and then only will war cease.

**1.54** This is the ultimatum presented to us: secure the conditions whereby men will entrust their security to a larger entity, or risk annihilation; persuade men that their salvation rests in the subordination of national and local interests to the interest of humanity, or endanger man's future.

**1.55** These are the objectives, yesterday unobtainable, today essential, which we must labor to achieve. Until this is accomplished, mankind's future remains hazardous and permanent peace, a matter of speculation.

**1.56** In order that the work of evil may not triumph again over this redeemed humanity, all peace-loving peoples must rally together for the definite re-establishment of right and peace.

**1.57** Today men hope for a special future, when yesterday we sought only the means to postpone the final holocaust.

**1.58** If the condition of peace is such as will satisfy the conscience and sense of justice of men, if it is assured to humankind that they shall toil and live happily under a just system in which no discrimination will be made between small and great, the peace system that shall be laid down can leave a heritage for coming generations which will be full of happy life and boundless prosperity.

**1.59** Man is basically a creature of peace.

**1.60** Use your knowledge for good, to preserve peace among men.

# Chapter 2 – Education

**2.1** We are determined to be masters of our fate; owners of our wealth; and capable of removing the adjective dark from the name of our continent. Education - that of the nation and of the individual - is the bastion of this goal.

**2.2** Knowledge paves the way to love, and love in its turn fosters understanding, and leads one along the path of great common achievements.

**2.3** Loyalty inspires understanding and understanding cooperation; these are the clearest evidence of strength.

**2.4** The solid basis for all lies in education. It is education which allows people to live together, and makes them avoid the pitfalls of immorality and induces respect for the law. Truly, the attainment of these high aims is based on education, the helping of people to live together, to avoid indulgence, immorality and lawlessness.

**2.5** An awareness of our past is essential to the establishment of our personality and our identity as Africans.

**2.6** Education, work and diligence are the main foundation of our national existence.

**2.7** To command and to be commanded is the fruit of education and unity [of which] confidence is the result.

**2.8** Education of the youth is the surest guarantee for a better life.

**2.9** In all the countries we have visited, we have noted that education is the basis for the greatness, the power, the pride and prosperity of a nation.

**2.10** A well-informed public opinion is essential to the growth of political and social awareness. Only he who is informed can comment on his nation's development and only by such comment can errors be corrected and progress stimulated.

**2.11** The construction of edifices for required schools is not the real problem; the problem is to awaken the people to the need for such schools.

**2.12** The possession of degrees alone does not classify anyone as fully educated.

**2.13** The person who claims to know everything, as the scriptures say, is like 'sounding brass and tinkling cymbal.'

**2.14** Universities stand today as the most promising hope for constructive solutions to the problems that beset the modem world —

promises which prevent the peaceful cooperation of nations, problems which threaten the world and humanity with death and disaster.

**2.15** From the universities, must come men, ideas, knowledge, experience, technical skills and the deep humane understanding vital to fruitful relations among nations. Without these, world order, for which we have so long strived, cannot be established.

**2.16** A university is the fountain of learning; seek knowledge, and there you shall find it.

**2.17** A fundamental objective of the university must be the safeguarding and the developing of the culture of the people which it serves.

**2.18** From the universities, too, must come that ability which is the most valuable attribute of civilized men everywhere: the ability to transcend narrow passions and to engage in honest conversation; for civilization is by nature 'the victory of persuasion over force.'

**2.19** The mere existence of a fund of knowledge is not enough; unless knowledge is nurtured and nourished by devoted teachers and eager students alike, it will, like a pool of water following the rains, change its hue and slowly disappear.

**2.20** A school is to shape one's character; just as looking into a mirror could rid himself of the dirt that is on his person, likewise can one shape his character by education.

**2.21** Man would prefer to speak of his nation in terms of its educated men and women rather than by recounting the size of the population.

**2.22** It is understood that the independence of mind created by education individually will have as a result, the creation of an independently-minded nation.

**2.23** Humanity by nature is gifted to think freely, but in order that his free thought should lead him to the goal of liberty and independence, his way of thinking must be shaped by the process of education.

**2.24** The development of the resources of intelligence which education draws forth from our people - vital as it is - without moral inspiration and guidance, can never of itself work for the good of all.

**2.25** All the knowledge to be drawn from the fountainhead of education not only contributes to the well-being of mankind and to the performance of humanitarian deeds, but is also a veritable pillar upholding the liberty of the land.

**2.26** The catastrophe which was brought about by human hands during the past years can be avoided in the future by religion and hope in God which should be in the heart of the people. …This can be achieved by education which, if not born by the youth, the effort which is made for peace will be in vain.

**2.27** As the gospel tells us, "a house built upon strong foundations can never be overthrown by storms. Similarly, when people are built up with minds well formed by education and knowledge, no trial of whatever kind can conquer them."

**2.28** Education and the quest for knowledge stop only at the grave.

**2.29** From truth alone, are born liberty and only an educated people can consider itself as really free and master of its fate.

# Chapter 3 – Religion

**3.1** God's reasoning differs from that of man.

**3.2** It is only when a people strike an even balance between scientific progress, spiritual and moral advancement, that it can be said to possess a wholly perfect and complete personality.

**3.3** It is only when the human mind is guided by religion and morality, that man can acquire the necessary vision to put all his ingenious inventions and contributions to really useful and beneficial purposes.

**3.4** Progress without religion is just like a life surrounded by unknown perils and can be compared to a body without a soul.

**3.5** Discipline of the mind is a basic ingredient of genuine morality and therefore of spiritual strength.

**3.6** Now is the time when sincere belief in man's kinship to God must be the foundation for all man's efforts for enlightenment and learning - the basis for all understanding, cooperation and peace.

**3.7** Knowing that material and spiritual progress are essential to man, we must ceaselessly work for the equal attainment of both.

**3.8** Belief in the Creator is the surest foundation of any civilization.

**3.9** It is only with God's will that man can reach his ends.

**3.10** Man is mortal; each one of us here will, one day, face his maker and answer for his actions.

**3.11** Any monument to be left for our people, to be permanent, must be erected upon spiritual foundations.

# Chapter 4 – Character

**4.1** The acts by which we live and the attitudes by which we act must be clear beyond question. Principles alone can endow our deeds with force and meaning. Let us be true to what we believe, that our beliefs may serve and honour us.

**4.2** Loyalty inspires understanding and understanding cooperation; these are the clearest evidences of strength.

**4.3** Do not be the victims of temporary contentment and petty satisfactions. Aspire for worthwhile aims that shall be ideals for succeeding generations.

**4.4** Feel the needs of others more than your own.

**4.5** If we permit ourselves to be tempted by narrow self-interest and vain ambition, if we barter our beliefs for short-term advantage, who will listen when we claim to speak for conscience and who will contend that our words deserve to be heeded?

**4.6** Learn not only formal education but also a self-discipline that should be worth inheriting.

**4.7** As a father should bequeath not only wealth to his children, but also provide them with proper education, so that they may have a richer and fuller life, so should it be the duty of those for whom much has been done, to show gratitude.

**4.8** Let us not recoil in hatred against those who, even while protesting their freedom from bias and prejudice, reveal by their actions that the poison of discrimination has left its lasting effects, and by this reaction, reveal that we, no less than they, are susceptible to that virus which is called intolerance.

**4.9** One seldom minimizes the value of money earned by the sweat of the brow, however small it may be, but for the extravagant, even a huge amount of money is worthless.

**4.10** Whenever conflict arises between material and spiritual values, the conscience plays an important role, and anyone who suffers from a guilty conscience is never free from this problem until he makes peace with his conscience.

**4.11** It is only natural for man to strive toward a better life, to wish to educate his children while he himself was uneducated, to desire to shelter and clothe them while he himself was naked and scourged by the elements, to strive to spare them from the cruel diseases by which he himself was ravaged.

**4.12** When these ends [striving towards a better life] are realized at the expense of others, at the cost of their degradation and poverty, these desires, which are not intrinsically immoral or pernicious in themselves, must be frustrated, and the means by which these otherwise legitimate ends are sought to be attained, must be scorned and shunned.

**4.13** That which does not give respite, is the feeling of a guilty conscience.

**4.14** I have lived too long to cherish many illusions about the essential high-mindedness of men when brought into stark confrontation with the issue of control over their security and their property interests.

**4.15** There is nothing better one can leave behind than a worthy and memorable name...

**4.16** Where are we to look for our survival, for the answers to the questions which have never before been posed? We must look first to Almighty God, who has raised man above the animals and endowed him with intelligence and reason. We must put our faith in him, that he will not desert us or permit us to destroy humanity which he created in his image.

**4.17** We must look into ourselves, into the depth of our souls. We must become something we have never been and for which our education and experience and environment have ill prepared us. We must become bigger than we have been, more courageous, greater in spirit, larger in outlook. We must become members of a new race, overcoming petty prejudice, owing our ultimate allegiance not to nations but to our fellow men within the human community.

**4.18** Unless we find the requisite courage and fixity of purpose to rise above our petty selves; we shall be broken on the wheel of our own invention, slaves of our own despotism.

**4.19** The spirit of Africa...is deserving of the greatness which Africa demands of it. Let us prove ourselves worthy of it.

**4.20** He who suffers, conquers, and in the final resort, wins the crown of victory.

**4.21** Place principle above all else.

# Chapter 5 – Responsibility

**5.1** Man desires many things, but it is the individual's duty and responsibility to desire the proper things.

**5.2** A noble failure may be of more value than a petty success.

**5.3** Anyone who makes the wrong choices will be a burden, not only to himself but to future generations.

**5.4** Though life is short, one should live and act in such a way that his achievements will bring him and his country a good name forever. If he does not use his training for worthy ends, he will be an enemy to himself and an obstacle to others. He will, indeed, be sick while supposedly healthy and dead while still alive.

**5.5** The obligation to improve oneself does not cease simply because one has a regular job.

**5.6** Simply watching other people's achievements is a characteristic of a lazy man.

**5.7** There is no person in this world who is free from life's responsibility.

**5.8** One who does not contribute to his community and the coming generation remains to be a burden to his society and an object of ridicule to outside observers.

**5.9** It is not enough for the children of Ethiopia to be recipients of education. They should never forget that the responsibility for passing on this knowledge to others and of handing it over to the next generation rests on them.

**5.10** If the wealth of a person cannot be for the general welfare, what would he gain for himself and his offspring but grudge and hatred?

**5.11** To place all responsibility on the shoulders of one individual while others sit by idly by and seek only to criticize and find fault is ... to act contrary to the movement for progress and advancement of the country.

**5.12** A qualified man with vision, unmoved by daily selfish interests, will be led to right decisions by his conscience.

**5.13** A man who knows from whence he comes and where he is going will cooperate with his fellow human beings. He will not be satisfied with merely doing his ordinary duties but will inspire others by his good example.

**5.14** Records of the past reveal the great achievements of our forefathers. It is up to us to try to emulate them, for they will be standing in judgement of us.

**5.15** Those that have fallen on the battlefield have sacrificed themselves so that our future would be more secure. And we the living have the responsibility of living up to the sacrifice that they have made.

**5.16** To those who contribute willingly, who, in sweat and toil, work for the good of the nation, with little thought of self, to them will much be given, even to the governing of the land.

**5.17** Each man must repay what he has received from his country.

# Chapter 6 – Advice to Students

**6.1** The opportunity for education ... is not given ... for a fashion or a mode. It is given for a purpose, for a task, for a high responsibility ... for the benefit of our country and the coming generation.

**6.2** The person who, even while at school, realizes the needs of his country and has a proper sense of values and urgency will see what is needed, and will be able to fill it.

**6.3** Education is not an end in itself, but an aid to assist you to distinguish between good and evil, between the harmful and the useful.

**6.4** Education intensifies natural gifts and ability, but mere education, unless founded on a historical and cultural framework, will bear no fruits.

**6.5** Choose the means by which you can best exercise self-control and self-discipline. In this, you are now possessed with the most important weapon of training.

**6.6** Avoid having a bad reputation and be eager and energetic in your studies, be loyal to your country and obedient to your teachers, eschew lies and follow truth, respect good and be heirs of good work.

**6.7** A man who is proud in spirit will always have confidence in himself and his conscience will not reprimand him.

**6.8** If you are open-minded and ready to learn, there are many things which you can learn not only from books and instructors but from the very [experience] of life…itself.

**6.9** There are definitely many things which you can learn from the people. If you are guided by this principle, you will be surprised how pleasant life can be.

**6.10** Translate into the vernacular of the plough, the spade and the hoe, the lessons you have learned from your specialized training … If you cannot do this, your education would have been futile; the labour would have gone to fashion a ship without a rudder.

**6.11** It is more the inward eye than the possession of eyesight, which is necessary for the acquisition of education.

**6.12** A man who says "I have learned enough and will learn no further" should be considered as knowing nothing at all.

**6.13** Do you like to serve people? Are you happy to work with people? Are you doing your best? ... Ask yourselves these questions as often as you can.

**6.14** A man's happiness is to make his brother happy, and to serve his country.

**6.15** Knowledge is power. If it is not applied properly to create, let there be no doubts, it will destroy.

**6.16** Study and examine all but choose and follow the good.

**6.17** The knowledge you have acquired so far is no end in itself but a reminder for the further responsibilities that await you.

**6.18** In your future work, be ever mindful to prove yourselves worthy of trust.

**6.19** Let all that you do contribute to the ultimate benefit of your motherland and your fellow men.

**6.20** Let your work always be such that you can take pride in it, and if you do so, your country will have reason to be proud of you.

**6.21** Let usefulness be your hallmark today, not adolescence.

**6.22** Your hands once put to the plough, [should] not look back.

# Chapter 7 – Work

**7.1** There is neither shame nor disgrace in a day's work well and truly done, whatever the task and whatever the rank or status of the worker. The farmer and the labourer who have toiled diligently throughout the day have earned their bread and honest sleep.

**7.2** ...[T]he man, whatever his rank, who has spent his time in idleness, whose hand has been turned to little of profit or value during his working hours, has earned only the scorn and disdain of his fellowmen whom he has cheated.

**7.3** Have not those many nations which today are called "advanced" become so through toil and labour of their peoples?

**7.4** It is easy to begin but hard to finish.

**7.5** A mature mind and a wealth of experience are needed to decide upon the time and place where strength and skill may be most effectively combined.

**7.6** Strength may be useless where skill is required.

**7.7** There is no protection from the demand that a man's worth be assessed by his achievements.

**7.8** Money is an instrument, but there is no duty that can be fully accomplished with its mere persuasive power.

**7.9** It is better to till the land rather than to bicker on trivial matters.

**7.10** It is better to exploit effectively a small tract of land rather to proclaim being the owner of vast idle land.

**7.11** A purely materialistic art would be like a tree which is expected to bear fruit without flowering, sacrificing grace and beauty for mere utility.

**7.12** Your workmanship will be a monument to your name.

**7.13** Mere talk is the instrument of the lazy and will not take us anywhere.

**7.14** Unless a man undertakes more than he can possibly do, he will never be able to do all he can.

**7.15** A man has to strive in order to grow.

**7.16** Everything is bound to be accomplished with man as initiator and God as executor.

**7.17** Man, who is by nature selfish, must learn that only in serving others can he reach the full stature or attain the noble destinies for which God created him.

**7.18** To do one's job is one thing and to be indifferent in general and be critical of the work of others is another matter. The former requires competence, determination and wisdom, while the latter lacks these qualities.

**7.19** It is inappropriate to be a burden in any sort of work, especially in the works undertaken in the general interest of a country.

**7.20** Laziness is the sole breeder of sin, poverty and discontent.

**7.21** By what means can man's achievements in this world be best remembered? Many people believe that this could be done by the erection of physical and material structures; others believe that their works are in themselves, lasting monuments.

**7.22** We for our part, think that man's contributions which live to influence the life and progress of posterity, are the most permanent monuments that ever be erected.

**7.23** The most worthwhile sort of life is one of service.

**7.24** The reward for the job well done is not the recognition of others, or in public praise. Neither is it to be measured solely by the monetary return earned by the workman.

**7.25** [The reward for the job well done]…comes, rather, in the inner satisfaction that accompanies the knowledge that the work accomplished represents the best of which we are capable.

**7.26** The attainment of any one goal is never more than a temporary achievement. A mountain-top is reached; beyond, on the far slope, there are new lands to explore, and new peaks to scale.

**7.27** Progress and work have no boundaries.

**7.28** By working together as neighbours, by making use of the resources which can be brought to bear through programmes of national development, of mutual help and of international assistance, we may face the future with confidence, secure in the knowledge that we can render a good account for our days and for our labours.

**7.29** Ahead of us lie the hard, the difficult years, years when we must grapple with new sets of problems and face new hardships.

**7.30** There will be little festivity and few celebrations in these years. Our task is now to prove ourselves worthy of the lot which we have claimed as our own, capable of employing our talents and resources in the cause of Africa and the African peoples.

**7.31** The way will be perilous, sacrifices will be demanded of us, our labours may go unobserved and our triumphs unnoticed except to ourselves. [I]n the ultimate sense, this is wholly as it should be, for we are men and this is man's lot.

**7.32** Let us work together, arm in arm as brothers, that our progeny may live in peace and well-being, that posterity will honour our names and our achievements. This will suffice. This will be our victory. May almighty God grant it to us.

# Chapter 8 – Self Help

**8.1** No person is able to understand and solve one's own problem better than one's self.

**8.2** Let us set our goals too high; let us demand more of ourselves than we believe we possess.

**8.3** In our efforts to improve the standard of life of our peoples and to flesh out the bones of our independence, we count on the assistance and support of others. But this alone will not suffice and, alone, will only perpetuate Africa's dependence.

**8.4** We have passed the point where prayerful pleading serves any purpose other than to debase those who thereby abdicate any responsibility or power to influence events.

**8.5** We cannot always depend on others.

# Chapter 9 – Development

**9.1** Let us not be too proud to face...honestly and frankly, the fact that by standards of the modern world, the African peoples today are poor. Our poverty need not cover us with shame.

**9.2** We must not be too proud to recognize the fact of Africa's economic situation as it exists today...we must not be cast down or discouraged by the magnitude of the problems which face us. For Africa is potentially rich.

**9.3** Our task ... is to improve the economic lot of all African peoples, to raise them to a standard of living comparable to that enjoyed by the most highly developed regions of the world today. This is a task and a challenge which must be met.

**9.4** [Improving the economic lot of all Africans] touches all of us, all must labour and work for success in this endeavour.

**9.5** The ultimate resource of a nation is its people. Unless this resource is employed for the benefit of the nation, unless the latent good which it represents is exploited to the maximum extent for the common good, the nation will languish, poor in spirit, lacking in achievement.

**9.6** If a man is sick in one part of his body, his whole constitution is upset. It is the same with a people. Unless each man's life be complete, displaying education and prosperity, the people as a whole cannot share in a common flourishing existence, nor can it give its governing cause for pride.

**9.7** The means of destroying poverty and ignorance are work and education.

**9.8** There is no one in the world who does not cherish the hope of having his standard of living raised.

**9.9** It is a law of nature and history that the development of any people must proceed simultaneously on all fronts.

**9.10** Man must be educated; he cannot come to grips with or cope with or understand the modern world unless he has been taught about it.

**9.11** He must be assured of a minimum economic security: he cannot concern himself with matters going beyond the day-to-day satisfaction of his physical needs unless he is fed, clothed and sheltered, nor can he acquire a sufficient degree of social consciousness to be able to subordinate his own personal interests to the good of the nation and the development of its society.

**9.12** It is not enough that a nation desire development and economic maturity, any more than a child, in wishing, becomes a man...the child must crawl before it can run.

**9.13** Who would not be pleased to see his baby born as a five or ten year old youngster? But this is contrary to nature's plan...progress must proceed in stages.

**9.14** Unless each beam be sound, the whole structure of a house cannot be firm.

**9.15** A country that has a plan is aware of its requirements.

**9.16** It is one of the tragedies of our day, that while half of the world's population is wracked by a never satisfied hunger and remains poverty-stricken, disease-ridden and ignorant, vast amounts are spent by great powers on armaments, money which, if diverted to satisfying the basic human needs of the poorer people of the world, could transform their lives and restore to them their human dignity, their happiness in the present and their confidence and faith in the future.

**9.17** In order to speed our economic development, most of us require extensive financial assistance. We need not be ashamed of this fact, particularly when the poverty and ignorance from which our peoples suffer have been perpetuated through the deliberate and longstanding policies of others.

**9.18** Aid must be without strings...It is possible to influence positions and oblige adherence to this or that policy by economic pressure, but only at the expense of pride and dignity of those who thus renounce their birthright as free men, and the bill of sale carries the caveat: "revocable at will."

**9.19** If the great nations of the world desire our sympathy and support, they should assist us to become economically strong, for only then will our alliance with them be meaningful.

**9.20** We cannot rely solely on international morality.

**9.21** The benefits of an expanding economy must be enjoyed by all.

**9.22** Our concern is with the many and not the few.

**9.23** If humanity is led to a better observance of covenants - that are meant for orderly conduct of life - and if the progress of science is applied solely for human welfare, the increase of population will become not a burden but a matter of gratification.

**9.24** Disarmament must be achieved, not only because in this fashion will the threat of a world holocaust be dispelled, but, equally, because only through a drastic reduction in the military budgets of the great powers can the vast resources required to raise all of mankind to the level of free men be freed for these purposes.

**9.25** We cannot postpone the needs...hopes...aspirations of our peoples indefinitely.

**9.26** A mark of a worthy civilization is the willingness of those to whom much has been given to share their portion with those in need.

**9.27** In aiding the young...we demonstrate our hope and faith in the future.

**9.28** We have the sacred duty to our children to spare them the sacrifices which we have known.

**9.29** To build a modern state requires the concentrated strength and effort of each one of you. If we do not build the roads and bridges and schools, if we do not plough the fields and till the soil, if we do not carry on the trade and commerce of the nation, to whom shall we look to for the accomplishment of these tasks?

**9.30** Just as it is important to defend one's country, it is equally important to prepare oneself for the welfare of the nation.

**9.31** Political and economic progress should go hand in hand.

**9.32** Poverty, fear, ignorance and disease are not problems vanquished in the wake of scientific progress; they are the problems with which we struggle from day to day.

**9.33** Penetrate and discern the hidden resources and opportunities that a benevolent providence has spread before us, in challenge to prove ourselves worthy of the means for bringing them to full development.

**9.34** Landless people must have the opportunity to possess their own land.

**9.35** In an era when nations gather in concert to declare each nation's fundamental rights to freedom and equality, it is dismaying that the great majority of the world's population exists in the shadow of poverty and misery, often lacking the basic essentials of food and clothing, while their fellowmen in other parts of the globe enjoy a life of abundance, comfort and tranquillity.

**9.36** No greater victory can be won by the nations of today than the conquest of apocalyptic enemies that still ride mankind - poverty, disease and ignorance.

**9.37** The basic needs of men everywhere are the same.

**9.38** The union of the spiritual strength of the people with the material power of the independent nation provides the firm basis of our people to overcome the hardships and difficulties of life facing them in this world.

**9.39** Food for the body and food for the mind are both essential.

**9.40** Civilization can serve for both good as well as evil purposes. Experience shows that it has invariably brought great dividends to those who use it for good purposes while it has brought incalculable harm and damnation to those who use it for evil purposes.

**9.41** Be it understood that while we...are justly proud of our national heritage, we do not look backwards to find our national purpose, but forward to the full realization of our national goals.

**9.42** It is the duty of all mankind to make the maximum use of the gifts, ingenuities, capacities and resources which has been placed at its disposal.

**9.43** [Gifts, ingenuities, capacities and resources] are not ours to do with as we will; they have been given to us in trust that we may, following the example of the developed countries, apply them for the highest benefit to ourselves and to posterity, and each one of us has a sacred duty to fulfil this trust and to prove ourselves worthy of the confidence reposed in us.

**9.44** Those men who preceded you have set a high example...Take up where they left off, emulate them, build on the foundation which they have laid down, that your nation may advance in progress and enlightenment.

**9.45** Africa will no longer be the "unknown continent," for its human and material resources are beyond measure, and this great continent now stands on the verge of an economic, political and cultural development which, when realized, will be without parallel in history.

**9.46** It is only when man becomes master of his fate - able to determine his destiny - that he can be free from fears and inferiority. Such an individual or a nation stands respected by all.

**9.47** If we ponder deeply on our situation today, we shall find that...the resources are available; the nation's youth are gaining knowledge and acquiring experience; it is only necessary that we resolve to work with determination and diligence.

**9.48** Of all the good things of the world which are accomplished by the wisdom of men and which can only be realized by that wisdom, health is the divine gift which is to found above all by those who can take care to guard it well.

**9.49** If health fails, teaching, knowledge, life itself, all comes to naught.

**9.50** The forests, the mountains and the plains constitute wealth.

# Chapter 10 – Leadership

**10.1** Leadership does not mean domination. The world is always well supplied with people who wish to rule and dominate others. The true leader is of a different sort; he seeks effective activity which has a truly beneficent purpose. He inspires others to follow in his wake, and holding aloft the torch of wisdom, leads the way for society to realize its genuinely great aspirations.

**10.2** The art of leadership consists in the ability to make people want to work for you, when they are really under no obligation to do so.

**10.3** Leadership is required in all fields and no field is without its usefulness.

**10.4** Within his own sphere, each has the same opportunities for showing ability, and the same potential satisfactions, as has the leader of a government.

**10.5** Leaders are people who raise the standards which they judge themselves - and by, which they are willing to be judged. The goal chosen, the objective selected, the requirements imposed, are not merely for their followers alone.

**10.6** [Leaders] develop with consummate energy and devotion to their own skill and knowledge in order to reach the standards they themselves have set. This whole-hearted acceptance of the demands imposed by ever-higher standards is the basis of all human progress.

**10.7** Leaders have to submit themselves to a stricter self-discipline and develop a more exemplary character than is expected of others. To be first in place, one must be first in merit as well.

**10.8** A good leader...maintains a balance between emotional drive and sound thinking.

**10.9** Once a person has decided upon on his life work, and is assured that in doing the work for which he is best endowed and equipped, he is filling a vital need, what he then need...is faith and integrity, coupled with a courageous spirit, so that, no longer preferring himself to the fulfilment of his task, he may address himself to the problems he must solve in order to be effective.

**10.10** To lead, one must first learn to follow.

**10.11** It is by deeds rather than by words that you can most effectively inspire.

**10.12** Love, generosity and understanding are evidence of the administrative experience of any government.

# Chapter 11 – Justice & Equality

**11.1** He who seeks justice, knows the value of justice too.

**11.2** Justice is the fundamental axiom for the survival of freedom and government.

**11.3** All men stand equal before the law.

**11.4** Religion is personal; the state is for all.

**11.5** In a peace without justice, there shall be neither peace nor justice.

**11.6** Since in the scale of creation all men are born equal, it is imperative that all laws be equitable in their application. For what is the foundation of freedom and what are the reasons that men cherish it, if they are not equal before the law?

**11.7** The natural origin of every man being man himself and thus being equal through creation, the only difference lies in the opportunities made available.

**11.8** The honour and interest of all persons depend on the wisdom of the laws, whereas humiliation, shame, iniquity and the denial of man's rights, all originate from the absence or inadequacy of laws.

**11.9** He who is worthy of praise amongst men is the man who, animated by sentiments of justice, perseveres in the way of equity.

**11.10** Unless the rights of the least of men are as assiduously protected as those of the greatest, the seeds of confidence will fall on barren soil.

**11.11** Honesty means not to oppress anybody and deny him his deserved share.

**11.12** When we speak of the betterment of man's life, we mean not merely the economic improvement of living standards; we refer, in addition, to the spiritual conditions in which man lives, for just as a man without means to feed his hunger and to clothe his nakedness can take no pride in his existence as a human being, so also is one who is reviled and discriminated against because of his race or religion, robbed of his self-respect and human dignity.

**11.13** The basis of racial discrimination and colonialism has been economic, and it is with economic weapons that these evils have been and can be overcome.

**11.14** Racial discrimination, by the nature of its aftermath, like a sleeping volcano, is capable of erupting anytime.

**11.15** Racial discrimination means the negation of the moral equity of all men and the deprivation of the African of his dignity and personality.

**11.16** We can never rest content with our achievements so long as men...assert on racial grounds their superiority over the least of our brothers.

**11.17** Racial discrimination constitutes a negation of the spiritual and psychological equality which we have fought to achieve and a denial of the personality and dignity which we have struggled to establish for ourselves as Africans.

**11.18** Until the philosophy which holds one race superior and another inferior, is finally and permanently discredited ad abandoned;

**11.19** … Until there are no longer first class and second class citizens of any nation;

**11.20** … Until the colour of a man's skin is of no more significance than the colour of his eyes;

**11.21** … Until the basic human rights are guaranteed to all without regards to race;

**11.22** … Until that day, the dream of lasting peace and world citizenship and the rule of international morality will remain but a fleeting illusion, to be pursued but never attained;

**11.23** … Until bigotry, prejudice, malicious and in-human self-interest have been replaced by understanding, tolerance and goodwill;

**11.24** … Until all Africans stand and speak as free beings, equal in the eyes of all men, as they are in the eyes of heaven;

**11.25** … Until that day, the African continent will not know peace. We Africans will fight, if necessary and We know We shall win, as We are confident in the victory of good over evil.

**11.26** As we do not practice or permit discrimination within Our nation, so We oppose it wherever it is found.

**11.27** As we guarantee to all the right to worship as he chooses, so We denounce the policy which sets man against man in the issues of religion. As we extend the hand of universal brotherhood to all, without regard to race or colour, so We condemn any social or political order which distinguishes among God's children…

**11.28** Man's ingratitude to man is often manifested in the willingness to relegate human beings to the scrapheap of life when they enter the twilight of their careers and younger brains and stronger arms are found to replace them.

**11.29** We Africans occupy a different – indeed a unique – position among the nations of this century. Having for so long known oppression, tyranny and subjugation, who with better right, can claim for all the freemen? Ourselves, for long decades, the victims of injustice, whose voices can be better raised in the demand for justice and rights for all?

**11.30** We must speak out on major world issues, courageously, openly and honestly, and in blunt terms of right and wrong. If we yield to blandishment or threats, if We compromise when no honourable compromise is possible, Our influence will be sadly diminished and Our prestige woefully prejudiced and weakened. Let Us not deny our ideals or sacrifice, Our right to stand as champions of the poor, the ignorant, and the oppressed everywhere.

**11.31** When no one upholds the cause of right and justice for their own sake, when the small still voice of conscience speaks no longer, immorality and lack of principle have triumphed, and in this, history and all of mankind is the loser.

**11.32** Let Us take pride in the fact that as free men We attack and abhor racial discrimination on principle, wherever it is found and in whatever guise.

**11.33** If We raise Our voices against injustice, wherever it be found, if We demand a stop to aggression wherever it occurs and under whatever guise and brand the aggressor as such, and if We do so on a wholly impartial basis, We can serve as the collective conscience of the world.

**11.34** Unflinching dedication to the charter is essential if world peace is to be strengthened and fundamental human rights are to be adequately safeguarded. In words and in deed, We must exemplify a resolute spirit to defend international morality when threatened and if necessary to suffer and die for truth and justice, so that this international morality will be reinforced and strengthened.

**11.35** If the condition of the peace is such as will satisfy the conscience and sense of justice of men, if it assured to human kind that they shall toil and live happily under a just system in which no discrimination will be made between small and great, then the peace system that shall be laid down, can leave a heritage for the coming generation, which will be full of happy life and boundless prosperity...

**11.36** The truth cannot be suppressed forever by false and subtle propaganda...

**11.37** If We preserve, discrimination will one day vanish from the earth.

# Chapter 12 – Unity & Brotherhood

**12.1** Wherever there is African blood there is a basis for greater African unity.

**12.2** The example of the developed countries amply proves the truth of the proverb, "Unity is strength."

**12.3** Our greatest asset is our unity, and we must exploit it to the fullest.

**12.4** People of a country who have fought incessantly for their independence, understand that unity is the foundation of liberty.

**12.5** The joining together in a unified effort to overcome the perils of nature and the dangers which beset man on all sides is the very basis of society and the way in which humanity, since the dawn of history, has assured its survival.

**12.6** We must remember that many states that today represent the major powers of the world were once weak, were once prey to other major forces. But, however, through the process of assimilation, through the process of the realization of fundamental national interests, and through the process of combination that they have achieved, they have become the major powers.

**12.7** When a solid foundation is laid, if the mason is able and his materials good, a strong house can be built.

**12.8** Africa must speak with one voice ringing out in powerful, harmonious tones.

**12.9** We are determined to create a union of Africans. In a very real sense, our continent is unmade; it still awaits creation and its creators. It is our duty and privilege to rouse the slumbering giant of Africa, not to the nationalism of Europe of the nineteenth century, not to regional consciousness, but bending its united efforts toward the achievement of a greater and nobler goal.

**12.10** Because the African people are dedicated to the cause of the maintenance of peace, because the African people are determined that there should be that material progress for their people, and because the African people believe in the essential precepts of democracy, these are the foundations of the Organization of African Unity.

**12.11** The fact that we succeeded in laying the foundation of our unity, was due primarily to the desire of all Africans to unite in a common struggle against colonialism, poverty, disease and ignorance, which are enemies of Africa.

**12.12** The nations of the world are today interdependent in such a way that the suffering or privation of any one is in greater or lesser measure a stricture on all others.

**12.13** Ten years ago, when Mussolini's Italy attacked our Empire, the masses of the world - even we would hazard, most individual members of the League of Nations - were in the fullest sympathy with us. ...[I]n the end, delay, discussions and considerations of the world prevailed.

**12.14** Help did not come...we can appreciate that true idealism may have lain behind those policies, now indeed regretted by the world and now admitted as disastrous, of "Peace at any price" and of "appeasement."

**12.15** ...We pray that unity and that the strength behind the unity, which failed before, will never lack again among the Councils of the world.

**12.16** In our age, man has replaced his individualistic attitude by a larger cause, namely the good of society.

**12.17** Men have started to think in terms of their fellowmen, their country and the world community. All must strive unceasingly to further these simple and yet fundamental principles and ideals so that there shall be a better tomorrow for generations to come.

**12.18** Each of us depends on the other, can learn from the other and in pursuing his own destiny, will go further and succeed more quickly with others.

**12.19** Influences abound which will not hesitate to divide us, to pit us one against the other and to stir up disharmony and suspicion where only brotherhood and confidence should be found.

**12.20** We have seen in the Congo the tragic consequences which follow when, within the confines of a single state, men who have been deprived of the concept of 'nation', whose horizons have been limited to the confines of their family relationships, are stirred up one against the other.

**12.21** Is Africa really fragmented, and has independence been achieved on this great continent only to see the African nations themselves transform differences into divisions? And are such divisions as already exist, imposed on us by history and circumstance, to be widened and deepened by our own efforts?

**12.22** Countries where the people and the entire country have lost unity, spiritual or otherwise, have become playgrounds and laughing stocks of outsiders.

**12.23** Nobody knows better than we Africans that the policy of divide and rule is the aspiration of those who seek to benefit at others expense.

**12.24** An age-old technique, which we may expect to encounter again and again in our struggle to attain independence in fact as well as in name, is summed up in the maxim "divide and conquer."

**12.25** The best chance for one country to attack another comes through noting the...divisions of its people within.

**12.26** It is a sound tactic of military strategy to attack where your opponent's defence is weakest. It is surely sound strategy for all of us to move ahead where such movement is unobstructed and unimpeded.

**12.27** A nation cannot prosper unless it has overcome the problems of communication. Without communication, agriculture cannot develop, nor can commerce or industry thrive. It is communication that relates and binds people together by ties of friendship.

**12.28** If we act where we may in those areas where action is possible, the inner logic of the programmes which we adopt will work for us and inevitably impel us still farther in the direction of ultimate union.

**12.29** For a man to remain isolated and separated from his neighbours and to have no access to the sources of knowledge and education is to remain prey to the ills and plague which afflict mankind in its primitive state.

**12.30** Do not fall into the narrowness which looks only to the borders of your nation...We must move ahead in concert with all mankind.

**12.31** Concerted action, cooperation, coordinated policies...are not just words, but great and noble conceptions. In them, and in what they stand for, can be found the key to fulfilment of the longings and the hopes of millions of Africans.

**12.32** Unity should be the cornerstone of relations among African states for it would ensure confidence and cooperation. Disunity, on the other hand, while dissipating their strength, always ends in regrettable results.

**12.33** Our greatest weapon is the oneness which we share as Africans.

**12.34** Strength can be achieved through unity, and success is the fruit of cooperation.

**12.35** Unity gives strength and assures success.

**12.36** No nation can divide within itself and remain powerful.

**12.37** Woe unto those countries which weaken themselves by dismemberment.

**12.38** We have no problem which is insurmountable...Let us work in unity and diligence.

**12.39** I have seen the progress of the people and I have seen their determination to march forward in unity towards greater progress.

**12.40** The tide which is sweeping Africa today cannot be stayed. No power on earth is great enough to halt or to reverse the trend. Its march is as relentless and inexorable as the passage of time.

**12.41** In the history of the human race, those periods which later appeared as great, have been the periods when the men and the women belonging to them had transcended the differences that divided them and had recognized in their membership, to the human race, a common bond.

**12.42** Sympathy and that spirit of brotherhood which constitutes a common bond among all Africans...has carried Africa forward in triumph on the crest of the wave in pursuit of the ideal of African unity and it remains unflagging today as we prepare for yet more vigorous efforts in the battle to win through to this cherished objective.

**12.43** There are those who claim that African unity is impossible, that the forces that pull us, some in this direction, others in that, are too strong to be overcome.

**12.44** Around us, there is no lack of doubt and pessimism, no absence of critics and criticism. These speak of Africa, of Africa's future and of her position in the twentieth century in sepulchral tones. They predict dissension and disintegration among Africans and internecine strife and chaos on our continent. Let us confound these and, by our deeds, disperse them in confusion.

**12.45** There are others whose hopes for Africa are bright, who stand with faces upturned in wonder and awe at the creation of a new and happier life, who have dedicated themselves to its realization and are spurred on by the example of their brothers to whom they owe the achievements of Africa's past. Let Us reward their trust and merit their approval.

**12.46** We encountered a sense of purpose, of dedication, of vision, which, we are persuaded, found its genesis in the common acceptance of the ideal of African unity, in the common response to the unique challenge which modem Africa presents to each of us, in the common crusade in which we are all enlisted.

**12.47** ...It is this spirit which will sweep us forward to final, conclusive, glorious victory in the struggle to overcome the obstacles which still remain before us in the making of a united Africa. It is in this, we believe, that the real triumph of Africa lies today.

**12.48** So long as the spirit of Africa prevails and stirs within us, so long as we continue to think and work and act within the African context which we have created, imbued by the African atmosphere which surrounds and pervades us, we are confident that the goals we seek shall be attained. We have created this spirit; it is our child.

**12.49** As Ethiopia is one, all Ethiopians are also one, and education is the only way to maintain this condition.

**12.50** Leave aside all misguided aims and groundless ambitions that can only lead us into wasteful and time-consuming conflicts. Let us instead mobilize our resources for our common good and for the good of our great continent. This is the heartfelt desire of African peoples everywhere, and it is the duty of us all always to bear this in mind and to strive for its full and final achievement.

**12.51** To meet together, to take council with one another, and to act in mutual cooperation, has proved a most fruitful method both in the secular and spiritual fields. Henceforth the way is open for you to follow this fruitful path.

**12.52** We shall find new ways to strengthen the links which already join our peoples and to advance arm in arm towards the happy future which is our hope not only for our own people but for all the world.

**12.53** Africa and African unity are more than mere words.

**12.54** As Solomon says, "physical distance cannot be a barrier to love".

**12.55** For the first time, Africa has learned what strength there is in unity.

**12.56** The distances among your respective countries have been abolished by the proximity of your hearts.

# Chapter 13 – Self-Defence

**13.1** How vital it is that men be jealous of their freedom.

**13.2** Our unity being our formidable weapon of defence, it should be kept more strengthened than our other forces of defence.

**13.3** It is not the heavy armour but the quality of the citizens that man it that matters.

**13.4** The value of a flag springs from the sacrifices made to defend it.

**13.5** Men of honour, whenever they may be, must be vigilant in defence of their freedom, so that they may be spared suffering and humiliation.

**13.6** No arms, however big or however mighty, can provide solace to a nation. A nation finds comfort, and the freedom of that nation is best protected, through the sacrifice and patriotism of its people.

**13.7** Even when faced with those who do not relent, continue to demonstrate love and consideration until obliged to resort to self-defence.

**13.8** Our strength resides not in the military might or in the economic wealth, but rather, in the cumulative moral influence which we can bring to bear on the peoples and the problems of the world.

**13.9** If those who would thrust the world into the holocaust of war are to be deterred from aggressive action. It can only be by the threat of a counterblow poised to strike - should the need arise.

**13.10** The pages of history are full of instances in which the unwanted and the shunned nonetheless occurred because men waited to act until too late.

**13.11** We are able to meet the demands of our time primarily because our ancestors, besides transmitting to us the benefits of tradition, had shed their blood to safeguard the independence and territorial integrity of our nation.

**13.12** In the dark hours when we and our people were called upon to fight, we did not fail in our fierce resolve...we have all earned the right to be proud of that heritage of struggle.

**13.13** We [do not] need...non-African assistance to defend our soil.

**13.14** Do not lament when you see a respected and beloved leader fall in the battlefield for the cause of our freedom. Instead, you must realise that anyone who dies for his country is indeed fortunate. Death comes to all whether in time of peace or war and takes those it chooses.

**13.15** Our forefathers preserved our country's independence through the sacrifice of their lives. Let them be your inspiration!

**13.16** The dead shall rest in peace for their sacrifice. [I]n defence of their country, [it] has been honoured.

**13.17** Men will die in defence of principle; men will sacrifice their all rather than compromise themselves and renounce that which distinguishes them from the beasts - their moral faculty. If this force in men can but be awakened and focused on the problems of each day, we shall, God willing, survive each day to the dawn of each tomorrow, and in this survival guarantee to our children and our children's children a lifetime of peace and security, under justice and right, and under God.

**13.18** We must save ourselves so we may be of service to others.

**13.19** It is better to die with freedom than without it.

**13.20** Unity is strength.

# Chapter 14 – Independence

**14.1** This world was not created piecemeal. Africa was born no later and no earlier than any other geographical area on this globe. Africans, no more and no less than other men, possess all human attributes, virtues and faults.

**14.2** Africa has been reborn as a free continent and Africans have been reborn as free men. The blood that was shed and the sufferings that were endured are today Africa's advocates for freedom and unity.

**14.3** Since freedom is an issue upon which national existence itself depends, it becomes a sacred obligation of primary importance for a people of one family, united in their own common life and in oneness of mind and spirit, to preserve their free and pleasant way of life from all external danger and thus be enabled to advance along the path of progress.

**14.4** The glories and advantages of freedom cannot be purchased with all the world's material wealth.

**14.5** Freedom's price is the sacrifice of the lives of innumerable heroes and, in deep realization of this; it becomes the duty of free men everywhere to be ever prepared for the defence of their freedom.

**14.6** Every nation that fights, as we have done, for the defence and maintenance of its independence has the right to expect the honour and indeed the assistance of all freedom-loving peoples.

**14.7** It is but natural that small nations, who must so vigilantly defend their independence, should regard collective security as the cornerstone of their existence. Their support of that principle should be instant, unhesitating and absolute. No small state, no democratic nation, no people imbued with charity towards its fellow men, could do otherwise.

**14.8** The strongest foundation of our independence is the development of our economic resources.

**14.9** Freedom, liberty, the rights of man, these mean little to the ignorant, the hungry, the ill clothed, the badly housed.

**14.10** Unless the political liberty for which Africans have for so long struggled is complemented and bolstered by a corresponding economic freedom and social growth, the breath of life which sustains our freedom may flicker out.

**14.11** Those who seek independence, must be prepared to struggle for it rather than accept it; and having won it, to stand on their own feet without dependence, and without favours.

**14.12** Each nation has an inherent right to shape its own destiny and to seek its own way to the high state of advancement which the free nations of the world have attained.

**14.13** A foreign hand is concerned about itself; it will not work for us.

**14.14** Independence cannot be a simple word devoid of meaning; it must remain a principle admitting of no compromise or suspicion, a principle demanding respect for self and at the same time equal respect for the rights of others.

**14.15** Our independence and freedom are meaningless unless they are tied to the hearts of our peoples.

**14.16** Those men who refused to accept the judgement passed upon them by the colonizers, who held unswervingly through the darkest hours to a vision of an Africa emancipated from political, economic, and spiritual domination will be remembered and revered wherever Africans meet.

**14.17** What we may utter today can add little to the heroic struggle of those who, by their example, have shown us how precious are freedom and dignity and of how little value is life without them. Their deeds are written in history.

# Chapter 15 – International Relations

**15.1** Apart from the Kingdom of the Lord, there is not on this earth any nation that is superior to any other.

**15.2** The perpetuation of the status quo will not, in the long run, serve even the narrow interests of the few, and it will inevitably prove disastrous to the world economic situation.

**15.3** It is, therefore, to be ardently hoped that the governments of the economically advanced countries will rise to this challenge and join in a concerted effort to alleviate the world's economic ills which are but the root and cause of many other international problems.

**15.4** Many learned men have on various occasions sought to abolish war and establish an everlasting peace. Treaties have been signed and organizations formed to achieve this goal, but because they lacked guarantees, these efforts uniformly failed, and to gain their ends, countries even resorted to the production and use of poison gas.

**15.5** Now nations are producing weapons, which not only constitute a terrible danger to those against whom they might be used, but in fact

71

could mean the end of mankind, and again there are no guarantees. If these awful weapons are used, who will bear the responsibility?

**15.6** If man has not sought out the protection of God as well as prepared himself for self-protection, the havoc and ruin that can be brought down upon the race of human beings is beyond the bounds of imagination.

**15.7** Global peace and security can only be permanently secured if all people of the world pool their resources towards the complete eradication of man's common enemies - ignorance, hunger and disease.

**15.8** Small nations ought to refrain from making themselves tools for igniting friction between the great powers. We must work together [to]…end…little wars which are consuming the energies of the small nations and decimating our people.

**15.9** Today the great powers should also wake up to the realization of the fact that the key to their destiny and future happiness does not lie in their own hands alone. There is no peace without cooperation.

**15.10** Be it known that the principle enshrined in the Charter and the resolutions adopted by the organization are not there only for the small nations to respect and to implement. In efforts being made to ease the gravity of world problems, the small nations should have a say. Their voices should be heard.

**15.11** Differences in economic and social systems should not give rise to mistrust and misunderstanding among nations. On the contrary, we should accept diversity in culture and tradition, and coexist peacefully.

**15.12** If we remain faithful to the principles of Bandung and apply them in our international life, we will maximize the influence which we can bring to bear on world problems.

**15.13** The American people can make a significant contribution to guaranteeing that a deep and abiding friendship exists between Africa and the United States of America.

**15.14** Learn more about us; learn to understand our backgrounds, our culture and traditions, our strengths and weaknesses. Learn to appreciate our desires and hopes, our problems, our fears. If we truly know one another, a solid and firm basis will exist for the maintenance of friendly relations...You may be assured that there will be no failure in the warm and brotherly response from our side.

**15.15** We are impressed by the achievement of the Japanese people in reaching a most advanced technology and creating a most flourishing economy without losing their ancient virtues nor their traditional personal and social values...Theirs is an example to be meditated upon and to be followed by other nations who are striving to solve their problems and to build their future in this troubled world.

**15.16** Cooperation among all nations of the world, east and west alike, is not only possible and desirable, but indispensable for the welfare of mankind.

**15.17** The stake of each one of us is identical - life or death. We all wish to live. We all seek a world in which men are freed of the burdens of ignorance, poverty, hunger and disease. And we shall all be hard pressed to escape the deadly rain of nuclear fallout should catastrophe overtake us.

**15.18** No system, not even that of collective security can succeed unless there is not only a firm determination to apply it universally, both in space and time, but also whatever the cost.

**15.19** Nowhere can the call for aid against aggression be refused by any state large or small. It is rather a universal principle or it is no principle at all.

**15.20** To be sure, there exists throughout the world a sense that something must be done and, as well, a belief that all that should be done is being done. But in terms of the enormous resources squandered in wars or in the amassing of weapons of destruction or even devoted to the enthralling conquest of space, the amount which is allotted to bettering the existence of the individual in the developing world, is little indeed.

**15.21** The sacrifices...and the long bitter struggle of our Empire for the defence and furtherance of the cause of collective security impose upon all nations alike the obligation rendered sacred by the lifeblood and sufferings of our people to ensure that war will not again sear the face of our fair lands, that justice and not expediency shall guide the councils of nations and, in the words of the Charter of the United Nations, "to reaffirm faith in fundamental human rights, in the dignity and worth of the human person and in the equal rights of nations large and small."

**15.22** The world is only now coming to realize what Ethiopia and Africa have long recognized, that peace, independence and prosperity of mankind can be achieved and assured only by the collective and united efforts of free men who are prepared to maintain eternal vigilance and labour unceasingly to protect these most precious of God's gifts.

**15.23** Those who lack the vision and foresight to realize that Africa is emerging into a new era, that Africans will no longer be denied the rights which are inalienably theirs, will not alter or reverse the course of history, but will not only suffer the inevitable consequences of their refusal to accept reality.

**15.24** In the midst of the strife and turmoil which marks Africa today, the African peoples still extend the hand of friendship. But it is extended to those who desire the progress and the political and economic freedom of African people, who are willing generously and without thought of selfish gain to assist us to our feet that we may stand by their side as brothers.

# Chapter 16 – United Nations

**16.1** The peoples of the world are about to succeed in overcoming the barriers of time and space by living as members of a closely linked family of nations as a result of the advances made by modern science and technology.

**16.2** It can be said, therefore, that the world has now reached the stage where matters affecting every individual country concern members of the entire international community. How best then could a world more united, peoples more intimately linked, attain the noble goal of further strengthening the spirit of international cooperation, establishing an atmosphere of mutual understanding and comprehension, and of making an effort for creating a world of supreme peace and happiness? The answer to this fundamental question must be provided by United Nations.

**16.3** It is perhaps, no accident that the United Nations headquarters resembles a structure of glass. It is a fragile, not an indestructible, institution.

**16.4** He who acts deliberately and with calculation to the injury of the United Nations, to weaken it or endanger its existence, is the enemy of all of us.

**16.5** We must, by force of circumstances, look to the United Nations, however imperfect, however deficient, to preserve the peace and to lend us its support in our endeavours to secure a better life for Our peoples, and we must concentrate our efforts, little or great, to the achievement of its stated ends, for only thus can we secure our free and continued existence.

**16.6** It is necessary that the governments of the United Nations who are now working for the reconstruction of the world peace, should be guided by the principles of impartiality so that they shall lay down a solid and proper foundation stone for a system of peace, which shall outlive generations.

**16.7** We live in an age of ideologies, and world peace is too precious a thing to be disturbed merely because of the clash of these ideologies. It is an entirely different matter, though, when one country attempts to interfere in the internal affairs of another.

**16.8** We believe that if all nations make the Charter of the United Nations the basis of their international relationships, all can live in peace and harmony in spite of their differences.

**16.9** The great powers, while prepared to use the United Nations when it suits their convenience, have been equally willing to ignore and bypass it and act independently of it when their interests so dictated.

**16.10** Unilateral action outside the United Nations is, however, a luxury denied to the poorer and weaker nations. But in the face of world opinion, massed in support of right and justice, we venture to suggest that even the great nations, powerful as they are, will hesitate.

**16.11** Let us not delude ourselves, it is not the great powers that need or benefit from the existence of the United Nations. It is the small powers, which depend on and require and demand that it live. It is we who have the most to gain through the successful achievement of its goals, it is we who have the most to lose should it one day be relegated to a tidy niche in history.

**16.12** The United Nations can only be effective, provided its members are willing to make it strong by giving their wholehearted support in each and every case where justice, decency and fair-mindedness so demand.

**16.13** The Charter of the United Nations expresses the noblest aspirations of man: abjuration of force in the settlement of disputes between states; the assurance of human rights and fundamental freedoms for all without distinction as to race, sex, language or religion; the safeguarding of international peace and security. But these, too, as were the phrases of the Covenant, are only words; their value depends wholly on our will to observe and honour them and give them content and meaning.

**16.14** The record of the United Nations during the few short years of its life, affords mankind a solid basis for encouragement and hope for the future.

**16.15** The United Nations...still provides the essential escape valve without which the slow build-up of pressures would have long since resulted in catastrophic explosion. Its actions and decisions have speeded the achievement of freedom by many peoples on the continents of Africa and Asia. Its efforts have contributed to the advancement of the standard of living of peoples in all comers of the world. For this, all men must give thanks.

**16.16** If we are to survive, the organization has got to survive.

# Chapter 17 – Our Past & Future

**17.1** To the Ethiopian people upon the surrender of the invading Italian forces:

Today is a day on which we defeated our enemy. Therefore, when we say let us all rejoice with our hearts, let not our rejoicing be in any other way but in the spirit of Christ. Do not return evil for evil. Do not indulge in the atrocities which the enemy has been practicing in his usual way, even up to the last moment. Take care not to spoil the good name of Ethiopia by acts which are worthy of the enemy. We shall see that our enemies are disarmed and sent the way they came...the aggressor and the persecutor are receiving their reward.

**17.2** It is they who are being driven out, while those they had oppressed and persecuted can now begin to wipe away their tears. Distorted history is changed to truth. The light of justice dawns again.

**17.3** Trusting in, and bragging of, the invincibility of this military force, the fascist government proceeded with planting totalitarian rule in our country. But something happened which the fascist government did not take into account: the fighting spirit which is essential in modem war, revealed in you.

**17.4** Those who had attacked us rejoiced in our defeat and in our tribulation. We trusted in the Lord. He gave us Victory. Our salvation is the Lord. Who here can fail to trust in God, whose judgements are all righteous and who fails not those who put their faith in him. Has not the Lord, the mightier than mighty, once again revealed that under the Kingdom of Heaven - no one Government of man is greater than another?

**17.5** The heroism, developed in the blood of our people and passed from generation to generation, has served to this day as a bulwark for our freedom, so that Ethiopia has never had to bear the yoke of slavery. To this, history and the world bear witness.

**17.6** We shall remember those heroic warriors who, determined not to surrender the great charge passed on to them by their Father, became sacrifices, shedding their blood and breaking their bones for the freedom of the land they loved and for the honour of their Emperor and their flag. The history of Ethiopia will be witness for these our warriors.

**17.7** Our people have earned through blood and tears the deep satisfaction gained with the restoration of a cherished and ancient independence.

**17.8** We must put to the best use the rich heritage of our past for, in that way, and in that way alone, can we live to the highest standard set by our forefathers.

**17.9** We hope the future generation will realize the magnitude of sacrifices that was required to accomplish all the works...so that it may preserve it as gain.

**17.10** It is a sad commentary, on the state of the world of that period, which tolerated the brutalities and the campaigns of unspeakable atrocities against Ethiopia.

**17.11** We ask, had the world refused to tolerate those immoralities, if it had reacted with energy against those violations of international law, might we not have been spared the countless deaths and sacrifices.

**17.12** Remember all those who have been hunted and murdered by the enemy.

**17.13** In a supreme moment of great historical vision, thirty African leaders undid the tangled knot of injustices bequeathed from long and shadowy years of colonialism. Thus...the Organization of African Unity born.

**17.14** In its wake, not only were vast vistas of challenges and opportunities opened, but also a stirring hope and sober recognition has dawned on Africa; a faith and a determination that, immense as are the challenges that lie ahead, they shall all be conquered, and abundant as are the opportunities that await us, they shall not be wasted.

**17.15** Africa is today at midcourse, in transition from the Africa of yesterday, to the Africa of tomorrow. Even as we stand here, we move from the past into the future.

**17.16** The task, on which we have embarked, the making of Africa, will not wait. We must act, to shape and mould the future and leave our imprint on events as they slip past into history.

**17.17** Change begets change...each step forward leads logically and inexorably to the next, and the next. Once unleashed, the forces of history cannot be contained or restrained, and he is naive indeed who says, "thus far I will go and no farther."

**17.18** Man may, at the outset, control the direction which events take, but once his choice is made, events soon escape his control and history proceeds by its own force and momentum.

**17.19** The problems which confront us today are...unprecedented. They have no counterparts in human experience. Men search the pages of history for solutions, for precedents, but there are none. This, then, is the ultimate challenge.

**17.20** What do we seek for Africa? We seek to consolidate and guarantee our own precious liberty as independent nations.

**17.21** We seek freedom for our still dependent brothers. We seek Africa's economic growth and development, the betterment of the way of life of Africans and all men.

**17.22** We seek the closest collaboration with those others - Asians, Europeans, North and South Americans - who share our desires and who are willing to cooperate with us.

**17.23** We seek that self-sufficiency which will enable us to play our rightful role in international affairs and live in full harmony with all men.

**17.24** We seek to make our voices heard and our views heeded on the major problems confronting the world today.

**17.25** Our quest, above all else, is to assure to Africa and to each African state, the fullest and most complete measure of freedom - freedom from all remnants of colonialism; freedom from neo-colonialism, whatever form it may take; freedom from political and military threat; freedom from aggression; freedom from interference by others in our internal affairs; freedom from economic domination; freedom from the danger of nuclear destruction. This is easy to state; how infinitely more difficult it is to achieve?

**17.26** There came an enemy who interrupted our peaceful work of leading Ethiopia to a high civilization and by invading our country, destroyed all the products of our work.

**17.27** Had it not been for all the various obstacles which we encountered and which hindered our work, it is obvious that the result of our initiative for the purpose of having Ethiopia combine her ancient civilization with the modem world progress would have appeared much earlier. Nevertheless, we thank God for the kindness we have never missed.

**17.28** Our nation has been tested and tempered with the cruel knowledge of experience and has emerged wiser and stronger for what she has undergone.

**17.29** Africa, like the rest of the world, is today, more than ever, passing through a transitional period from the Africa that was to the Africa that is to be. We have now begun to tread the path of the too future, and the task that we have set for ourselves to carry out in building a better and secure tomorrow for Africa, is an arduous one.

**17.30** The risks which history and circumstances have thrust upon us, deemed balanced and sober reflection. If we succeed at the tasks which lie before us, our names will be remembered and our deeds recalled by those who follow us. If we fail, history will puzzle at our failure and mourn what was lost.

**17.31** Our people of Ethiopia! Listen! Thanks be to God who is impartial to all, who can break the arms of the strong and who stands by the oppressed.

**17.32** Africa has come of age.

**17.33** We must, all of us, look beyond today.